ECOSYSTEM Changes

by Donna Latham

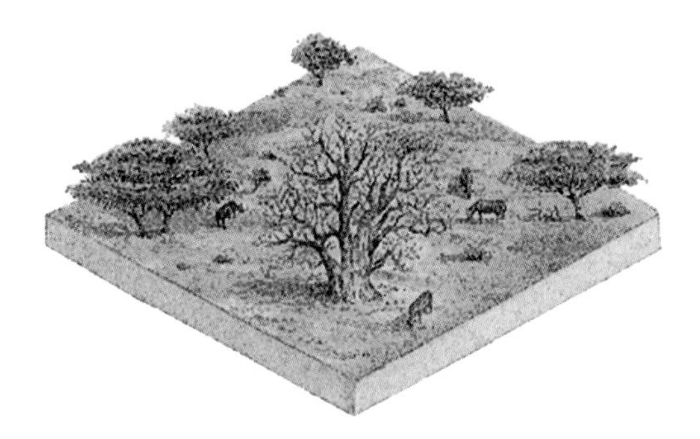

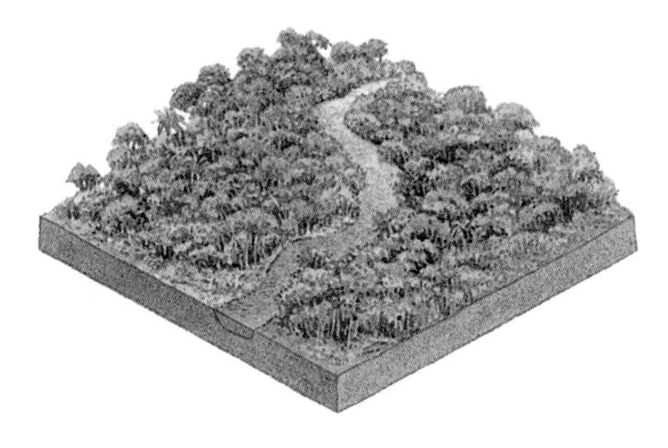

Balance on the Trail

You are hiking in Yellowstone National Park. It is the oldest national park in the world. It is also one of the biggest wildlife preserves in the United States. As you walk along the trail, you can observe the balance of nature. It's all around you.

Look—over there. That adult bull elk weighs close to one thousand pounds. Its striking, spreading antlers have twelve points. As you quietly observe, the elk grazes in the grasses beneath the trail. The largest herd of elk in the United States can be found here. At one time, elk could be found in the eastern forests and prairies of the United States. But they were hunted so much that they died out in many areas.

Now look above you. Do you see that huge flock of white pelicans? They soar high over the trail until they fly out of sight. They are going on a group fishing expedition to one of the park's lakes. There they will swim along the water's surface. Staying in a line, they will chase the fish to shallow water. Once the fish have been trapped there, the pelicans will scoop them up in their pouches and swallow them whole.

That is how the balance of nature works. Both the elk and the white pelican survive in Yellowstone National Park because the environment gives them everything they need to live. All their needs are met in a balanced ecosystem. Let's find out how!

Balanced Ecosystems

All living things depend on each other and their environment to live and grow. The ways in which they interact keep the ecosystem balanced.

One of this elk's needs is water.

What Living Things Need

Consider the elk you just saw along the hiking trail. Every day it depends on the living and nonliving things in the park to survive. Think about all the ways the environment meets the elk's needs. It gets food from the grasses and trees that grow there. These plants give oxygen, which the elk needs to breathe. Where do you think the elk gets the water it drinks? Yellowstone's rivers and lakes, as well as streams and ponds, supply water. And do not forget the puddles that rainwater supplies!

It's summer now, so the elk lives in the higher mountain areas. But in the winter, the elk and its herd will move to the lower valley. They will stay there together, where there is not much snow. Twigs from fir and juniper trees will provide food. By staying together in a herd, the elk will be protected from predators such as bears and wolves.

In order to grow and be healthy, all living things need food, water, and living space. They must also have shelter, light, and air. Organisms also need the right soil and the right kind of weather conditions. Living things survive in environments that meet all of their needs.

Elk also need air and living space.

Staying Balanced

To stay healthy, ecosystems must be balanced. All living things in an ecosystem are connected. If something happens to just one thing, all the parts of the ecosystem are affected. Suppose that you have balanced a pyramid of oranges on your desk. What would happen to the pile if you removed one orange from the middle? Everything would move and shift. The whole pile might tumble down. That is the way the balance of nature works too.

In order for an ecosystem to be balanced, the food supply, living space, and shelter for a group of animals must be just right. Let's investigate the balance of three living things in Yellowstone—the weasel, the rabbit, and the clover plant.

The clover, rabbit, and weasel each play a role in the balance of their ecosystem. In order to live, clover needs sunlight, water, and minerals from the soil. It also needs space. Rabbits need clover so they can live and grow. By eating clover, rabbits help keep it from taking up space that other plants need. By preying on rabbits, the weasel makes sure that the rabbit population does not get too big. That way, the clover is not completely eaten up. Other plants and animals rely on the clover for oxygen and moisture. That keeps them all alive.

In a balanced ecosystem, there is always change. First, organisms are born. Then they live and die. After death they decompose. With these changes constantly taking place, an ecosystem can remain balanced.

The Cycle of Change and Balance

Many changes cancel each other out. For example, one rabbit may fall prey to a weasel, and elsewhere another rabbit may be born. When water dries up from a puddle, it is replaced during the next rainstorm. Animals use oxygen from the ecosystem when they breathe. As plants grow, they put oxygen back into the ecosystem.

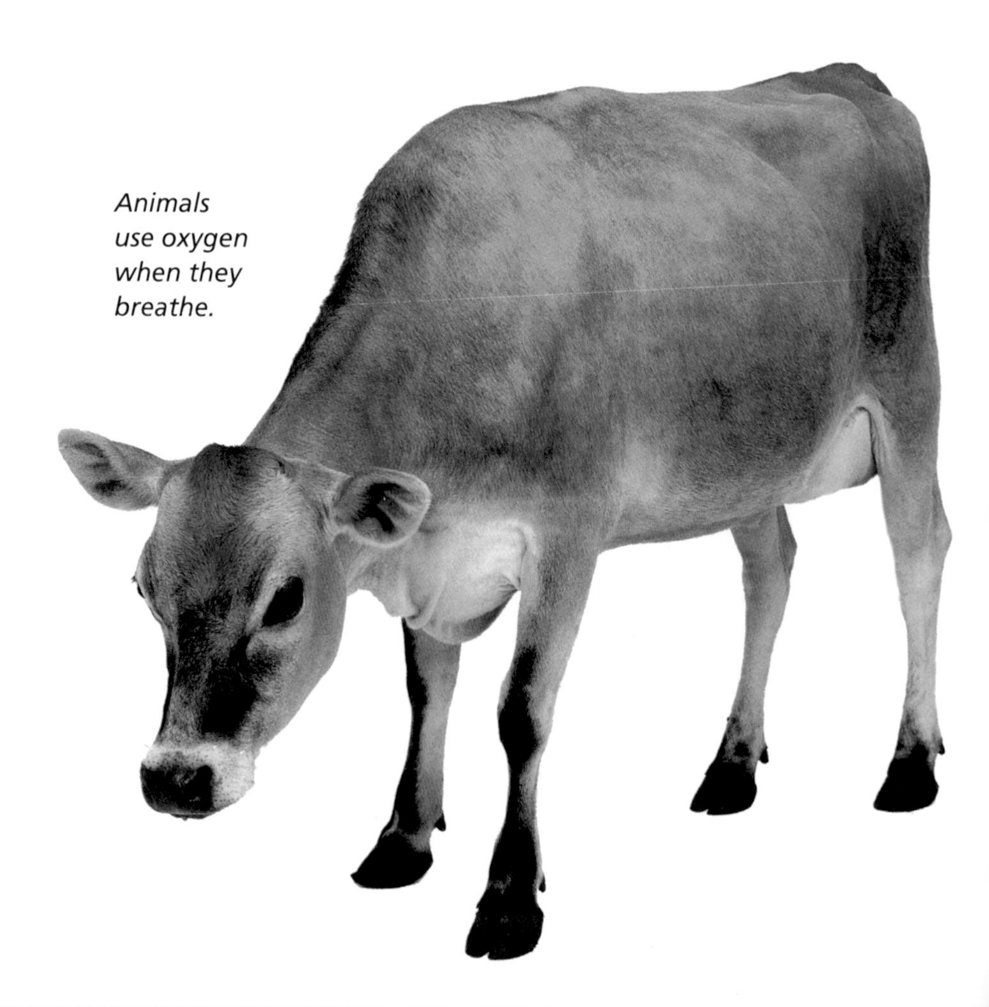

Animals use oxygen when they breathe.

Organisms Interact

Within an ecosystem, organisms compete for resources. But competition is just one way organisms can interact.

Changing Ecosystems

Plants and trees give off oxygen.

When the number of resources in an ecosystem changes, populations change too. Think about the rabbit. With plenty of clover and other plants to eat, it can live and grow. More rabbits enter the ecosystem. But extra rabbits require extra plants for food. They need living space and water too. In time, the rabbit population might use up all these resources. The rabbits will die or move away from the area. When more rabbits move into a new area, they will find plenty of resources. The cycle will begin again in a new location. The rabbits will do well in their new environment, because their needs are met. Their population will expand again. Eventually this new location will not be able to meet their needs. What might happen then?

Competition

In an ecosystem, organisms must compete for and share resources. **Competition** is the struggle between two or more species to use the same limited resources. Every organism has its own adaptations that help it compete for resources. Successful adaptations help organisms live and grow.

Living space is a survival requirement. It is also a source of competition. Different plant species compete for water and sunlight. Some plants grow tall, for example, and choke out others. Birds compete for the same prime locations to build their nests. Have you ever seen a blue jay? This bird, with its blaring call, actually takes over other birds' nests. During nesting seasons, it tosses eggs from other nests and moves in.

blue jay

lynx
cougar

Animals behave in special ways to decrease competition or to avoid it completely. Consider the canine and feline predators of Yellowstone National Park. Both groups prey on small mammals, including squirrels, rabbits, and mice. These two groups of predators hunt in different ways. The canines include wolves, coyotes, and foxes. With their strong bodies and quick running abilities, they hunt in wide-open areas. The feline predators, including the bobcat, cougar, and lynx, hunt in woody areas. Since their hunting style is based on sneak attacks, they use plants to help hide them from their prey.

Living in Harmony

Organisms can live together and help each other. The peony plant and some ants have a helpful relationship. The peony has a waxy outer covering on its bud. If this covering becomes too thick, it can prevent the bud from opening. Ants get energy by eating the coating off the bud. The ants acquire food from the peony, and the peony cannot bloom without the ants.

Parasites and Hosts

Not all the interactions in an ecosystem are helpful. One organism may help itself while it harms another. The organism that is helped is a **parasite.** The organism that is often hurt is the **host.**

In Yellowstone, a microscopic parasite attacks the cartilage in cutthroat trout. It becomes difficult for the trout to feed, and they die. As the trout decompose, they release spores of the parasite into the water. Those spores find new hosts.

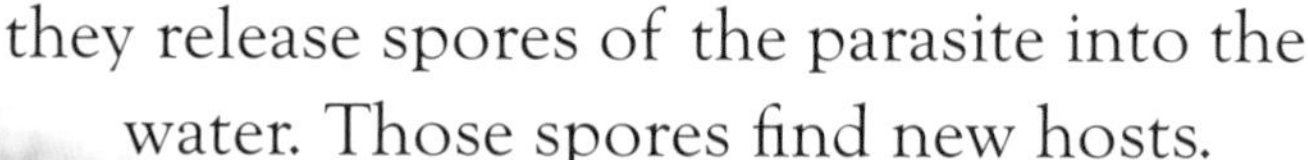

Changing Environments

Environments naturally change. This can happen very slowly or very quickly. When an environment changes, ecosystems and their species can be affected.

A forest you might live near or have visited may have changed over time. Thousands of years ago, it may have been a lake. Over time that lake dried up, and a marsh took its place. As more time passed, trees, grass, and bushes replaced the marsh, creating a forest.

Succession is the gradual change from one community of organisms to another. As an environment changes, succession takes place. In most cases, it takes place in stages. Communities will grow and take over for one another. Eventually, one community will become another kind of community.

The Stages of Succession

Succession takes place over time. Climate changes, such as warmer or colder weather, can influence how quickly succession occurs.

Bare land is often the starting point. The land provides weeds and some herbs, which help the soil.

In time, grasslands grow. Shrubs and grasses begin to spread over the land.

Shrubs continue to grow, making way for pine trees. Over time, oak and hickory trees begin to replace the pine trees.

Finally, a mature forest fully replaces the shrub land.

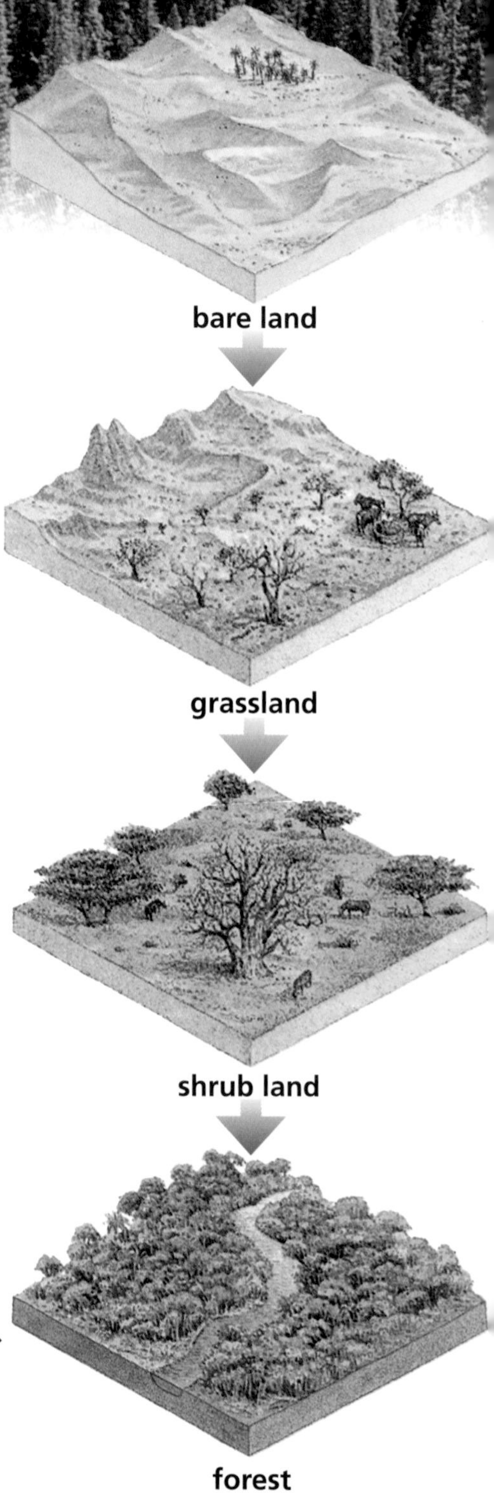

bare land

grassland

shrub land

forest

How Species Change

You know that dinosaurs are extinct. Did you realize that many other animals are extinct too? When an animal is **extinct,** the entire species has died out. It is gone forever. Species become extinct for different reasons. Climate changes, volcanoes, meteorites, and human activities may have caused extinction.

The woolly mammoth is extinct. Its size was much larger than that of a modern-day Asian elephant. It was covered with a warm coat that protected it from cold temperatures. Scientists believe that most woolly mammoths died out about eleven thousand years ago, partly due to changes in their environment.

The Steller's sea cow is another extinct animal. Once there were nearly two thousand of them in the Bering Sea. But sailors hunted them for food. The Steller's sea cow died out by 1768, less than thirty years after it was discovered.

Endangered Species

When the population of a species has become very low, that species is endangered. An **endangered** species is in danger of becoming extinct. Species that might soon become endangered are called threatened species. Sometimes endangered and threatened species leave an environment. They try to find a place where they can survive.

The black-footed ferret of the western United States is an endangered animal. Once there were many of them. They eat prairie dogs and, similar to the weasels they are related to, slip into burrows to capture their prey. But ranchers thought the prairie dogs were pests, and they began to kill them. With their food supplies running low, the black-footed ferrets began to die.

Scientists thought that all the black-footed ferrets had died out. But when a group of them were discovered in Wyoming, scientists acted quickly. They captured the population and cared for the ferrets in captivity. Since 1991, captive-bred black-footed ferrets have been returned to the wild.

Species Past and Present

Have you ever seen a fossil? Fossils are important clues to Earth's past. They let us know that life on Earth has not always been the way it is now. Over long periods of time, species have changed or adapted. Changes in their environment caused them to do so. Today, scientists compare fossils of organisms to organisms that are alive today.

What do you know about sharks? You may know that some species of shark have a huge set of jaws. This allows them to capture and devour their prey. Now think about this puzzle. Scientists discovered a bizarre set of teeth from the *Helicoprion*, an ancient shark. It lived 250 million years ago in waters off North America, Japan, and Australia, among other places. What makes the set of teeth bizarre is that they are in a spiral shape, much like the shape of a circular saw. Scientists are still working to figure out just how this set of buzz-saw teeth fit in the shark's mouth.

Rapid Natural Changes

Quick changes in a habitat can affect species that live there. Think of extreme weather events. A hurricane's strong winds can rip up trees and tear down plants. Heavy rains and huge waves can flood a community. Lightning can strike a tree and start a fire that wipes out everything in its path. These natural events can take resources away from the species that need them.

But rapid events do not only cause harm. They also play an important part in keeping an ecosystem balanced. Fires clear away dead plant matter. They make room for new plants to grow. Flooded areas help fish populations grow.

People and the Environment

Like other organisms, people interact with their environment. We get water, food, and shelter there. But unlike other organisms, we can change the environment to meet our needs. For example, we clear land to build houses or roads. We cut down trees. When we change the environment, we can upset the balance of ecosystems.

The waste products we make disturb ecosystems too. We pollute the air and water with these products. With our cars and factories, we release harmful chemicals into the air. Plants can die from those chemicals. The animals that need those plants might lose their food and shelter. When one action takes place, it affects others.

Water Pollution

When wastes and chemicals get into lakes, rivers, and oceans, our water becomes polluted. Some substances get into the water through sewer systems. Some chemicals are useful for killing insects or helping plants grow, but they can be harmful too. Rain washes the chemicals from the land into our water. These chemicals can kill fish and other animals and plants that live in the water.

Sometimes when oil is being drilled or shipped, it is spilled. The ocean's plant and animal inhabitants, such as this sea bird, can be harmed.

Land Pollution

Garbage, litter, and other things pollute our land. Did you know that in the United States every person produces about two kilograms, or about four and one-half pounds, of garbage each day? Most of that trash is dumped into landfills and covered up with soil.

Land pollution also occurs in the disposal of hazardous wastes. **Hazardous wastes** are substances that can hurt humans and other organisms. They can be poisonous or cause diseases. They can even start fires.

At one time, hazardous wastes were placed into barrels and buried. But some of the wastes leaked out. They damaged the habitats where they were buried. Today, laws require that hazardous waste disposal follow strict rules.

Strip Mining

Strip mining is a way of getting coal from under Earth's surface. Big machines dig up layers of soil to get to the coal. This leaves behind huge holes. Rocks and soil are swept into ponds and rivers, upsetting those ecosystems. Now there are laws that require mining companies to put back the rocks and soil that they removed. This is called reclamation. It helps restore habitats.

You have learned that living things depend on one another and on their environments. You know that changes in an environment will affect all living things that inhabit it. It is true of the environment in Yellowstone National Park. And it is true of your own environment as well!

Glossary

competition the struggle between organisms to meet their needs or to use the same resources

endangered at risk of dying out

extinct totally died out

hazardous wastes materials that are harmful to people and other organisms, as well as to the environment

host an organism that provides food or shelter to another living thing

parasite an organism that lives on or in another living thing and often harms it

succession the process of one community taking the place of another over time